Conjure

Books by Ishmael Reed

Novels

The Free-Lance Pallbearers (Doubleday, 1967)
Yellow Back Radio Broke-Down (Doubleday, 1969)
Mumbo Jumbo (Doubleday, 1972)

Anthology

19 Necromancers From Now (Doubleday, 1970)

Ishmael Reed

Conjure

Selected Poems, 1963-1970

University of Massachusetts Press

Library of Congress Catalog Card Number 72-77568
Printed in the United States of America

Designed by Richard Hendel

Some of these poems have appeared before in *Catechism of D
NeoAmerican HooDoo Church* (London: Paul Breman); *Umbra,
Black World (Negro Digest), Liberator, Essence, Ikon, Scholastic*
and *For Now* magazines; Anthologies: *In A Time of Revolution,
Where's Vietnam?*, and *Poets of Today*, edited by Walter Lowenfels;
The Poetry of the Negro, 1745–1970, edited by Langston Hughes
and Arna Bontemps; *The New Black Poetry* edited by Clarence
Major; *Soulscript*, edited by June Meyer Jordon; *The Norton
Anthology of Poetry*, Arthur M. Eastman, Coordinating Editor.
"The Neo-HooDoo Manifesto" was first published in the *L. A. Free
Press* newspaper. A slightly different version of "Badman of the
Guest Professor" appears in Dudley Randall's *The Black Poets* and
Adam David Miller's *Dices*.

For my pal Steve Cannon
And in fondest remembrance
Of my agent and friend
Abe Friedman
One of a vanishing breed
Humanist, individual, gentleman

Foreword

I wrote my second poem at the age of 14 (1952) while serving time at Buffalo Technical High School, Buffalo, New York. (The principal was a six-foot math teacher with broad shoulders.) A rhyme, its subject was Christmas. Earlier my mother and her co-sales women at Statler's Department Store, on Fillmore Avenue, in Buffalo, commissioned me to write a poem celebrating a fellow employee's birthday. I rose to the occasion with another rhyme.

I didn't write another poem until dropping out of college in 1960. Swept away by the "wide gap between the social classes," I moved into Buffalo's notorious Talbert Mall Project (a horrible experience, the only friendly event being the birth of my daughter, Tim). A period of political activism was followed by one of cynicism. I took part in a political campaign, writing publicity, registering voters, and knocking on doors, in the snow; on behalf of a black councilman. (It turned out that he had secretly thrown the election for a bigger job.)

All of my early attempts at poetry were lost in an old car abandoned on the freeway while I was enroute to New York (1962).

"The Ghost of Birmingham" (1963) shows the influence of people I studied in college: Yeats, Pound and the prosey typography is similar to that found in Blake's "The Marriage of Heaven and Hell." (Excuse me. I know that it's white culture. I was a dupe, I confess.)

"The Jackal-Headed Cowboy" (1964) was written under the influence of Umbra Workshop, the institution which began the current inflorescence of "Black poetry" as well as many other recent Afro-American styles of writing. (Umbra Workshop's role has been neglected by Johnny-Come-Lately "critics" who doctored the photos to show themselves standing next to the Emperor.)

"Jackal . . ." attempts to mix images and symbols from the cultures of Europe and Africa and Afro-America. (Egypt is located in Africa, you know, even though certain Western Civ. fanatics pretend that it lay in the suburbs of Berlin.)

"Gangster's Death" (March 1966) was written under pure inspiration as if the loas were whispering in my ear. If America had listen to me then, her son, her prophet, much of the agony of the following years could have been avoided. Christian countries never heed necromancers (formerly nigromancers [don't ask me]); are even hostile to them. "Philo Judaeus makes Saul say, that if he banishes from the land every diviner and necromancer his name will survive him."* If the government ever created a Bureau of Prophesy, Saul and his cronies would certainly stack it.

"The feral pioneers" was written while my wife and I were starving in Berkeley, California (1967); unsophisticated nATiOnaLIStS denied me a teaching job when I refused to end my lectures with Sieg Heil!! Perceptive people will notice that certain images are derived from the Donner Pass episode; Marcia Herskovitz will notice more than that.

"Badman of the guest professor" was written while I taught in Seattle, Washington (Winter 1969). Although the "straight" "square" "upright" Americans gave me every consideration and courtesy, radical/liberals were as evil as they could be. They didn't like me because I couldn't, like John Carlos, run around the track a few times or didn't have a rapist's past history; behaving like something romping about the rooftops, looking crazy, in "The Murders in the Rue Morgue." One of them, because I wasn't teaching his kind of reading list, mischievously placed a copy of the *MLA Style Sheet* among my student's textbooks at the bookstore. (I found its discussion of the semicolon to be quite weak.) Unlike Jackie Robinson, who, when a similar incident occurred, petted the black cat tossed onto the field, next to where he was seated on the bench; I boiled the black cat in a poem until it was down to its simmering mojo. The result was "Badman . . . ."

Poems such as this one will show that I am at home with malice (in the African tradition Kongo satirists were feared because they had a habit of putting their enemies' names "in a song"). I am equally at home with Legbaism (Eros to some), and "sublime" love. "catechism of d neoamerican hoodoo church" (1968) was written because I got sick of brawl-

* *Isis Unveiled,* Vol. I., H. P. Blavatsky.

ing in the streets with the Zombies of Ideology. "catechism
. . ." was something, being zombies, they could relate to. As a
fetishmaker it was necessary for me to return to my ancient
protection. I found "psychic self-defense" to be much hipper
than "put-up-your-dukes." Classier too.

"Mojo Queen of the Feathery Plumes," "The Black Cock,"
"Betty's Ball Blues," and "The Wardrobe Master of Paradise," completed in the fall of 1970, were set to music by
Ortiz Walton, a bassist, formerly with the Boston Symphony.*
We made a mastertape of the songs with me reading, Ortiz
playing bass, and celebrated VooDooist Marcus Gordon on
drums.

No record company would handle them. Ravi Shankar's
producer turned them down saying, "There's too much
black magic in the world already." New York record com-
panies complained that they were not enough like *The Last
Poets* (us can be only one thing), and Ralph Gleason of
Fantasy Records said they weren't "exciting." (How come
black people always have to be "exciting"?)

Except for "catechism . . ." which was begun in New York
the remainder of the poems were written while living in the
West, sometimes employed at the University of Washington
at Seattle or the University of California at Berkeley. "Neo-
HooDoo Manifesto" was first published in the *Los Angeles
Free Press,* (September 18–24, 1970) and reprinted in Quincy
Troupe's *Confrontation* magazine (Vol. II). It was the first attempt to define ancient Afro-American HooDoo as a con-
temporary art form. For those refractory West Civ. types,
black and white, who might be nauseated by the argument,
cheer up; it is followed by two gumbo recipes from Marie
Laveau's cookbook from the late 1800's. Let these be your
tonic.

The last poem "introducing a new loa," points to what I am
doing now.

Berkeley, California   Ishmael Reed
February 1972

* Charles Munch wanted to make him Concert-Master.

Contents

xi

Conjure

The Ghost in Birmingham

The only Holy Ghost in Birmingham is Denmark Vesey's Holy Ghost, brooding, moving in and out of things. No one notices the figure in antique cloak of the last century, haunting the pool games, talking of the weather with a passerby, attending mass meetings, standing guard, coming up behind each wave of protest, reloading a pistol. No one notices the antique figure in shabby clothing, moving in and out of things—rallies of moonshine gatherings—who usurps a pulpit and preaches a fire sermon, plucking the plumage of a furious hawk, a sparrow having passively died, moving in and out of chicken markets, watching sparrow habits become hawk habits, through bar stools and greenless parks, beauty salons, floating games, going somewhere, haranguing the crowds, his sleeves rolled up like a steel worker's, hurling epithets at the pharoah's club-wielding brigade, under orders to hunt down the first born of each low lit hearth.

There are no bulls in America in the sense of great symbols, which preside over resuscitation of godheads, that shake the dead land green. Only the "bull" of Birmingham, papier maché, ten dollars down monthly terms, carbon copy mock heroic American variety of bullhood, who told a crowded room of flashbulbs that there was an outsider moving in and out of things that night, a spectre who flashed through the night like pentecost.

He's right, there was.

Not the spook of the Judaic mystery, the universal immersed in the particular. Not the outsider from unpopular mysteries, a monstrous dialectic waddling through the corridors of his brain, but the nebulous presence hidden by flashbulbing events in Birmingham, Metempsychosis stroking the air.

Pragma the bitch has a knight errant called Abbadon, in the old texts the advocate of dreadful policies. The whore, her abominations spilling over, her stinking after-births sliming their way towards a bay of pigs, has a bland and well-groomed knight errant who said that "if we hand down a few more decisions, pile up paper, snap a few more pictures by

Bachrach of famous people before grand rhetorical columns of the doric order, perhaps they will stop coming out into the streets in Raleigh, Greensboro, Jackson and Atlanta (sometimes called the Athens of the south).

Pragma's well-groomed and bland procurer is on long distance manufacturing heroes,
Heroes who bray in sirens screaming in from Idlewild, winging in from points south,
Their utterances cast into bronze by press-card-carrying harpies, those creatures of distorted reality.

O ebony-limbed Osiris, what clown folk singer or acrobat shall I place the tin wreath upon?
When will Osiris be scattered over 100 ghettoes?

Heroes are ferried in by motorcycle escorts, their faces cast into by Pointillism, by Artzybasheff,
Sculptor of Henry Luce's America.

Introducing the King of Birmingham, sometimes called the anointed one,
And receives the tin wreath across Americana banquet rooms,
His hands dripping with blood like a fanatical monk as rebellion squirms on the stake.

Introducing the Black Caligula, who performs a strip tease of the psyche,
Between Tiffany ads and Vat 69, giving up a little pussy for a well-groomed and bland knight errant.

O ebony-limbed Osiris, what knight club tap dancing charlatan shall I place the tin wreath upon?
All things are flowing said the poet when gods ambushed gods:
Khan follows Confucius
Light follows darkness
Tin wreathed heroes are followed by the figure in antique clothes, obscured by the flash-bulbing events in Birmingham.
Metempsychosis in the air.

The Jackal-Headed Cowboy

We were - clinging to our arboreal - rustled
by a poplin dude so fast that even now
we mistake big mack trucks flying
confederate crossbones for rompaging
steer, leaping into their sandpaper hides
and lassoing their stubble faced drivers as they roar into
corn flaked greasy spoons.

We span the spic and spanned cesspools
nerves rankling like hot headed guerillas
bayoneting artery routes and crawling through
our bowels with blades in their teeth.

Our mohair suits, our watches, our horn
rimmed glasses and several telephones
petition us to slow down as we forget
whose soupcan we swim.

We stand at Brooklyn Bridge like
mayakovsky before, deafened by the nuts
and bolts and clogged in the comings and
goings of goings of Usura

We are homesick weary travelers in the
jungian sense and miss the brew of the
long night's pipe.

Our dreams point like bushy mavericks to
hawking game and scattering ripple falls.
We will swing from giant cables as if
they were hemp, hacking away at sky
scrapers til they tumble into christmas
crowds.
We will raid chock full O nuts untying
apron strings crouching stealthily in the streets
breaking up conference rooms sweeping away
forms memo pads, ransoming bank presidents
shoving dollar bills through their mahogany
jaws.

We will sit on Empire Sofas listening to
Gabrieli's fortissimo trumpets blare for
stewed and staggering Popes as Tom Tom mallets
beat the base of our brains.
We will leap tall couplets in a single bound
and chant chant Chant until our pudgy swollen
lips go on strike.
Our daughters will shake rattle roll and slop
snapping their fingers until grandfather
clocks' knees buckle and Tudor mansions free
their cobwebs.
Our mothers will sing shout swing and foam
making gothic spires get happy clapping the
night like blown up Zeppelin.

We will sizzle burn crackle and fry like combs
snapping the naps of Henri Christopher's daughters.
and We will scramble breasts bleating like
some tribe run amuck up and down desecrating
cosmotological graveyard factories.
and We will mash stock exchange bugs til
their sticky brown insides spill out like
reams of ticker tape.
and We will drag off yelling pinching bawling
shouting pep pills, detergents, acne powders,
clean rooms untampered maiden heads finger bowls
napkins renaissance glassware time subscriptions
reducing formulas
- please call before visiting -
- very happy to make your acquaintanceship i'm sure -
and boil down one big vat of unanimal stew
topped with kegs and kegs of whipped dynamite
and cheery smithereens.
and then We will rush like crazed antelopes
with our bastard babies number books mojo goofer
dusting razor blades chicken thighs spooky ha'nts
daddygracing fatherdivining jack legged preaching
bojangles sugar raying mamas into one scorching
burning lake and have a jigging hoedown with the

Quadrilling Sun.
and the panting moneygrabbing landlord
leeching redneck judges will scuffle
the embankment and drag the lipstick sky outside.
and their fuzzy patriarchs from Katzenjammer orphic
will offer hogmaws and the thunder bird and their overseers
will offer elixir bottles of pre punch cards
and the protocol hollering thunder will announce
our main man who'll bathe us and swathe us.
and Our man's spur jingles 'll cause the clouds to
kick the dust in flight.
And his gutbucketing rompity bump will
cause sweaty limp flags to furl retreat
and the Jackal-headed cowboy will ride reins
whiplashing his brass legs and knobby hips.
And fast draw Anubis with his crank letters from Ra
will Gallop Gallop Gallop

our mummified profiled trail boss
as our swashbuckling storm fucking mob rides shot
gun for the moon and the whole sieged stage coach
of the world will heave and rock as we
bang stomp shuffle stampede cartwheel and cakewalk our
way into Limbo.

The Gangster's Death

how did he die/ O if i told you,
you would slap your hand
                 against your forehead
and say good grief/ if I gripped you
by the lapel and told how they dumped
      thalidomide hand grenades
into his blood stream and/
              how they injected
a cyst into his spirit the size of an egg
which grew and grew until floating
      gangrene encircled the globe
and/ how guerillas dropped from trees like
mean pythons
          and squeezed out his life/
so that jungle birds fled their perches/
so that hand clapping monkeys   tumbled
      from branches and/
how twelve year olds snatched B-52's
      from the skies with their bare hands and/
how betty grable couldn't open a hershey bar
      without the wrapper exploding and/
how thin bent women wrapped bicycle chains
      around their knuckles saying
      we will fight until the last bra or/
      give us bread or shoot us/ and/
how killing him became child's play
in Danang in Mekong in Santo Domingo

        and how rigor mortis was sprinkled
in boston soups
              giving rum running families
stiff back aches
so that they were no longer able to sit
at the elbows of the president
with turkey muskets   or/ sit
on their behinds watching the boat races
off Massachusetts through field glasses but/
how they found their duck pants

pulled off in the get-back-in-the-alleys
of the world and/
how they were routed by the people
spitting into their palms
just waiting to use those lobster pinchers
or smash that martini glass and/
how they warned him
and gave him a chance
with no behind the back dillinger
killing by flat headed dicks but/
how they held megaphones
in their fists
saying   come out with your hands up and/
how refusing to believe the jig was up
he accused them
of apocalyptic barking
saying out of the corner of his mouth
come in and get me and/
how they snagged at his khaki legs
until their mouths were full
of ankles and calves and/
how they sank their teeth into his swanky jugular
getting the sweet taste of max factor
on their tongues and/
how his screams were so loud
that the skins of eardrums blew off
and blood trickled
down the edges of mouths

and people got hip to his aliases/
i mean/
democracy and freedom began bouncing
all over the world
like bad checks
as people began scratching their heads
and stroking their chins
as his rhetoric stuck in his fat throat
while he quoted

men with frills on their wrists
and fake moles on their cheeks
and swans on their snuff boxes
    who sit in Gilbert Stuart's portraits
    talking like baroque clocks/
    who sit talking turkey talk
to people who say   we don't want
             to hear it
as they lean over their plows reading Mao
wringing the necks of turkeys
    and making turkey talk gobble
    in upon itself
in Mekong and Danang and Santo Domingo
and

Che Guevara made personal appearances everywhere

Che Guevara in Macy's putting incendiary flowers
on marked down hats   and women
scratching out each other's eyes over ambulances
Che Guevara in Congress putting TNT shavings
in the ink wells   and politicians
tripped over their jowls trying to get away
Che Guevara in small towns and hamlets
where cans jump from the hands of stock clerks
    in flaming super markets/
where skyrocketing devil's food cakes
    contain the teeth of republican bankers/
where the steer of gentleman farmers
    shoot over the moon like beefy missiles
                 while undeveloped people
stand in road shoulders saying
fly Che fly bop   a few for us
    put cement on his feet
    and take him for a ride

O Walt Whitman
visionary of leaking faucets

great grand daddy of drips
    you said I hear america singing
but/ how can you sing when your throat is slit
and O/ how can you see when your head bobs
        in a sewer
in Danang and Mekong and Santo Domingo

and look at them weep for a stiff/
                                    i mean
a limp dead hood
Bishops humping their backsides/
folding their hands in front of their noses
forming a human carpet for a zombie
men and women looking like sick dust mops/
    running their busted thumbs
    across whiskey headed guitars/
weeping into the evil smelling carnations
    of Baby Face McNamara
    and Killer Rusk
whose arms are loaded with hijacked rest
in peace wreaths and/
look at them hump this stiff in harlem/
sticking out their lower lips/
and because he two timed them/
        midget manicheans shaking their fists
        in bullet proof telephone booths/
        dialing legbar on long distance
        receiving extra terrestrial sorry
                            wrong number
seeing big nosed black people land in space ships/
seeing swamp gas/
shoving inauthentic fireballs down their throats/
bursting their lungs on existentialist rope skipping/
        look at them mourn/
drop dead egalitarians and CIA polyglots
    crying into their bill folds
    we must love one another or die

while little boys wipe out whole regiments with bamboo sticks
while wrinkled face mandarins store 17 megatons in Haiku

for people have been holding his death birds
on their wrists and his death birds
make their arms sag with their filthy nests
and his death birds at their baby's testicles
and they got sick and fed up
with those goddamn birds
and they brought their wrists together and blew/
                                        i mean/
puffed their jaws and blew and shooed
   these death birds his way
and he is mourned by
drop dead egalitarians and CIA polyglots and
midget manicheans and Brooks Brothers Black People
   throwing valentines at crackers
   for a few spoons by Kirk's old Maryland engraved/
   for a look at Lassie's purple tongue/
   for a lock of roy roger's hair/
   for a Lawrence Welk champagne bubble

as for me/ like the man said
i'm always glad when the chickens come home to roost

x

The feral pioneers

for Dancer

I rise at 2 a.m. these mornings, to
polish my horns; to see if the killing
has stopped. It is still snowing outside;
it comes down in screaming white
clots.

We sleep on the floor. I popped over
the dog last night & we ate it with
roots & berries.

The night before, lights of a
wounded coyote I found in
the pass.
(The horse froze weeks ago)

Our covered wagons be trapped
in strange caverns of the world.
Our journey, an entry in the thirty-
year old Missourian's '49 Diary.
    'All along the desert road from the
    very start, even the wayside was strewed
    with dead bodies of oxen, mules & horses
    & the stench was horrible.'

America, the mirage of a
naked prospector, with sand
in the throat, crawls thru
the stink.
Will never reach the Seven Cities.
Will lie in ruins of
once great steer.

I return to the cabin's
warmest room; Pope Joan is
still asleep. I lie down, my hands
supporting my head.

In the window, an apparition,
Charles Ives:
tears have pressed white hair
to face.

Instructions to a princess

for tim

it is like the plot of an ol
novel. yr mother comes down
from the attic at midnite & tries
on weird hats. i sit in my study
the secret inside me. i deal it
choice pieces of my heart. down
in the village they gossip abt
the new bride.
i have been saving all this
love for you my dear. if my
house burns down, open my face
& you will be amazed.

There's a whale in my thigh

There's a whale in my thigh. at
nite he swims the 7 seas. on
cold days i can feel him sleeping.
i went to the dr to see abt myself.
'do you feel this?' the dr asked,
a harpoon in my flesh. i nodded
yes in a clinic room of frozen
poetry.
'then there's no whale in yr thigh.'

there's a whale in my mind. i
feed him arrogant prophets.

I am a cowboy in the boat of Ra

'The devil must be forced to reveal any such physical evil
(potions, charms, fetishes, etc.) still outside the body
*and these must be burned.' (*Rituale Romanum, *published*
1947, endorsed by the coat-of-arms and introductory
letter from Francis cardinal Spellman)

I am a cowboy in the boat of Ra,
sidewinders in the saloons of fools
bit my forehead   like   O
the untrustworthiness of Egyptologists
who do not know their trips. Who was that
dog-faced man? they asked, the day I rode
from town.

School marms with halitosis cannot see
the Nefertiti fake chipped on the run by slick
germans, the hawk behind Sonny Rollins' head or
the ritual beard of his axe; a longhorn winding
its bells thru the Field of Reeds.

I am a cowboy in the boat of Ra. I bedded
down with Isis, Lady of the Boogaloo, dove
down deep in her horny, stuck up her Wells-Far-ago
in daring midday getaway. 'Start grabbing the
blue', I said from top of my double crown.

I am a cowboy in the boat of Ra. Ezzard Charles
of the Chisholm Trail. Took up the bass but they
blew off my thumb. Alchemist in ringmanship but a
sucker for the right cross.

I am a cowboy in the boat of Ra. Vamoosed from
the temple i bide my time. The price on the wanted
poster was a-going down, outlaw alias copped my stance
and moody greenhorns were making me dance;
    while my mouth's
shooting iron got its chambers jammed.

I am a cowboy in the boat of Ra. Boning-up in
the ol West i bide my time. You should see
me pick off these tin cans whippersnappers. I
write the motown long plays for the comeback of
Osiris. Make them up when stars stare at sleeping
steer out here near the campfire. Women arrive
on the backs of goats and throw themselves on
my Bowie.

I am a cowboy in the boat of Ra. Lord of the lash,
the Loup Garou Kid. Half breed son of Pisces and
Aquarius. I hold the souls of men in my pot. I do
the dirty boogie with scorpions. I make the bulls
keep still and was the first swinger to grape the taste.

I am a cowboy in his boat. Pope Joan of the
Ptah Ra. C/mere a minute willya doll?
Be a good girl and
bring me my Buffalo horn of black powder
bring me my headdress of black feathers
bring me my bones of Ju-Ju snake
go get my eyelids of red paint.
Hand me my shadow

I'm going into town after Set

I am a cowboy in the boat of Ra

look out Set   here i come Set
to get Set   to sunset Set
to unseat Set   to Set down Set

                    usurper of the Royal couch
                    imposter RAdio of Moses' bush
                    party pooper O hater of dance
                    vampire outlaw of the milky way

18

Black power poem

A spectre is haunting america—the spectre of
  neo-hoodooism.
all the powers of old america have entered into a holy alli
ance to exorcise this spectre: allen ginsberg timothy leary
richard nixon edward teller billy graham time magazine the
new york review of books and the underground press.

may the best church win. shake hands now and come
out conjuring

Neo-HooDoo Manifesto

Neo-HooDoo is a "Lost American Church" updated. Neo-HooDoo is the music of James Brown without the lyrics and ads for Black Capitalism. Neo-HooDoo is the 8 basic dances of 19-century New Orleans' *Place Congo*—the Calinda the Bamboula the Chacta the Babouille the Conjaille the Juba the Congo and the VooDoo—modernized into the Philly Dog, the Hully Gully, the Funky Chicken, the Popcorn, the Boogaloo and the dance of great American choreographer Buddy Bradley.

Neo-HooDoos would rather "shake that thing" than be stiff and erect. (There were more people performing a Neo-HooDoo sacred dance, the Boogaloo, at Woodstock than chanting Hare Krishna . . . Hare Hare!) All so-called "Store Front Churches" and "Rock Festivals" receive their matrix in the HooDoo rites of Marie Laveau conducted at New Orleans' Lake Pontchartrain, and Bayou St. John in the 1880's. The power of HooDoo challenged the stability of civil authority in New Orleans and was driven underground where to this day it flourishes in the Black ghettos throughout the country. Thats why in Ralph Ellison's modern novel *Invisible Man* New Orleans is described as "The Home of Mystery." "Everybody from New Orleans got that thing," Louis Armstrong said once.

HooDoo is the strange and beautiful "fits" the Black slave Tituba gave the children of Salem. (Notice the arm waving ecstatic females seemingly possessed at the "Pentecostal," "Baptist," and "Rock Festivals," [all fronts for Neo-HooDoo]). The reason that HooDoo isn't given the credit it deserves in influencing American Culture is because the students of that culture both "overground" and "underground" are uptight closet Jeho-vah revisionists. They would assert the American and East Indian and Chinese thing before they would the Black thing. Their spiritual leaders Ezra Pound and T. S. Eliot hated Africa and "Darkies." In Theodore Roszak's book *The Making of a Counter Culture*—there is barely any mention of the Black influence on this culture even though its members dress like Blacks talk like Blacks walk like Blacks, gesture like

Blacks wear Afros and indulge in Black music and dance
(Neo-HooDoo).

Neo-HooDoo is sexual, sensual and digs the old "heathen"
good good loving. An early American HooDoo song says:

Now lady I ain't no mill man
Just the mill man's son
But I can do your grinding
till the mill man comes

Which doesnt mean that women are treated as "sexual toys"
in Neo-HooDoo or as one slick Jeho-vah Revisionist recently
said, "victims of a raging hormone imbalance." Neo-HooDoo
claims many women philosophers and theoreticians which
is more than ugh religions Christianity and its offspring
Islam can claim. When our theoretician Zora Neale Hurston
asked a *Mambo* (a female priestess in the Haitian VooDoo)
a definition of VooDoo the Mambo lifted her skirts and ex-
hibited her Erzulie Seal, her Isis seal. Neo-HooDoo identifies
with Julia Jackson who stripped HooDoo of its oppressive
Catholic layer—Julia Jackson said when asked the origin of
the amulets and talismans in her studio, "I make all my own
stuff. It saves money and it's as good. People who has to buy
their stuff ain't using their heads."

Neo-HooDoo is not a church for egotripping—it takes its "or-
ganization" from Haitian VooDoo of which Milo Rigaud wrote:

Unlike other established religions, there is no heirarchy of
bishops, archbishops, cardinals, or a pope in VooDoo. Each
oum'phor is a law unto itself, following the traditions of Voo-
Doo but modifying and changing the ceremonies and rituals in
various ways. Secrets of VooDoo.

Neo-HooDoo believes that every man is an artist and every
artist a priest. You can bring your own creative ideas to
Neo-HooDoo. Charlie "Yardbird (Thoth)" Parker is an example of the Neo-HooDoo artist as an innovator and improvisor.

In Neo-HooDoo, Christ the landlord deity ("render unto Cae-

21

sar") is on probation. This includes "The Black Christ" and "The Hippie Christ." Neo-HooDoo tells Christ to get lost. (Judas Iscariot holds an honorary degree from Neo-HooDoo.)

Whereas at the center of Christianity lies the graveyard the organ-drone and the cross, the center of Neo-HooDoo is the drum the anhk and the Dance. So Fine, Barefootin, Heard it Through The Grapevine, are all Neo-HooDoos.

Neo-HooDoo has "seen a lot of things in this old world."

Neo-HooDoo borrows from Ancient Egyptians (ritual accessories of Ancient Egypt are still sold in the House of Candles and Talismans on Stanton Street in New York, the Botanical Gardens in East Harlem, and Min and Mom on Haight Street in San Francisco, examples of underground centers found in ghettos throughout America).

Neo-HooDoo borrows from Haiti Africa and South America. Neo-HooDoo comes in all styles and moods.

Louis Jordon Nellie Lutcher John Lee Hooker Ma Rainey Dinah Washington the Temptations Ike and Tina Turner Aretha Franklin Muddy Waters Otis Redding Sly and the Family Stone B.B. King Junior Wells Bessie Smith Jelly Roll Morton Ray Charles Jimi Hendrix Buddy Miles the 5th Dimension the Chambers Brothers Etta James and acolytes Creedance Clearwater Revival the Flaming Embers Procol Harum are all Neo-HooDoos. Neo-HooDoo never turns down pork. In fact Neo-HooDoo is the Bar-B-Cue of Amerika. The Neo-HooDoo cuisine is Geechee Gree Gree Verta Mae's *Vibration Cooking*. (Ortiz Walton's Neo-HooDoo Jass Band performs at the Native Son Restaurant in Berkeley, California. Joe Overstreet's Neo-HooDoo exhibit will happen at the Berkeley Gallery Sept. 1, 1970 in Berkeley.)

Neo-HooDoo ain't Negritude. Neo-HooDoo never been to France. Neo-HooDoo is "your Mama" as Larry Neal said. Neo-HooDoos Little Richard and Chuck Berry nearly succeeded in converting the Beatles. When the Beatles said they were more popular than Christ they seemed astonished at the resulting outcry. This is because although they could feebly through amplification and technological sham 'mimic' (as if Little Richard and Chuck Berry were Loa [Spirits] practicing ventriloquism on their "Horses") the Beatles failed to realize that they were conjuring the music and ritual (although imitation) of a Forgotten Faith, a traditional enemy of Christianity which Christianity the Cop Religion has had to drive underground each time they meet. Neo-HooDoo now demands a rematch, the referees were bribed and the adversary had resin on his gloves.

The Vatican Forbids Jazz Masses in Italy
Rome, Aug. 6 (UPI)—The Vatican today barred jazz and pop-ular music from masses in Italian churches and forbade young Roman Catholics to change prayers or readings used on Sundays and holy days.

It said such changes in worship were "eccentric and arbi-trary."

A Vatican document distributed to all Italian bishops did not refer to similar experimental masses elsewhere in the world, although Pope Paul VI and other high-ranking churchmen are known to dislike the growing tendency to deviate from the ac-cepted form of the mass.

Some Italian churches have permitted jazz masses played by combos while youthful worshipers sang such songs as "We Shall Overcome."

Church leaders two years ago rebuked priests who per-mitted such experiments. The New York Times, August 7, 1970.

Africa is the home of the loa (Spirits) of Neo-HooDoo al-though we are building our own American "pantheon." Thou-sands of "Spirits" (Ka) who would laugh at Jeho-vah's fury concerning "false idols" (translated everybody else's religion) or "fetishes." Moses, Jeho-vah's messenger and zombie swiped the secrets of VooDoo from old Jethro but neverthe-less ended up with a curse. (Warning, many White "Black de-lineators" who practiced HooDoo VooDoo for gain and did not "feed" the Black Spirits of HooDoo ended up tragically. Bix Beiderbecke and Irene Castle (who exploited Black Dance in the 1920s and relished in dressing up as a Nun) are examples of this tragic tendency.

Moses had a near heart attack when he saw his sons dancing nude before the Black Bull God Apis. They were dancing to a "heathen sound" that Moses had "heard before in Egypt" (probably a mixture of Sun Ra and Jimmy Reed played in the nightclub district of ancient Egypt's "The Domain of Osiris"— named after the god who enjoyed the fancy footwork of the pigmies).

The continuing war between Moses and his "Sons" was recently acted out in Chicago in the guise of an American "trial."

I have called Jeho-vah (most likely Set the Egyptian Sat-on [a pun on the fiend's penalty] Satan) somewhere "a party-pooper and hater of dance." Neo-HooDoos are detectives of the metaphysical about to make a pinch. We have issued warrants for a god arrest. If Jeho-vah reveals his real name he will be released on his own recognizance de-horned and put out to pasture.

A dangerous paranoid pain-in-the-neck a CopGod from the git-go, Jeho-vah was the successful law and order candidate in the mythological relay of the 4th century A.D. Jeho-vah is the God of punishment. The H-Bomb is a typical Jeho-vah "miracle." Jeho-vah is why we are in Vietnam. He told Moses to go out and "subdue" the world.

There has never been in history another such culture as the Western civilization—a culture which has practiced the belief that the physical and social environment of man is subject to rational manipulation and that history is subject to the will and action of man; whereas central to the traditional cultures of the rivals of Western civilization, those of Africa and Asia, is a belief that it is environment that dominates man. The Politics of Hysteria, *Edmund Stillman and William Pfaff.*

"Political leaders" are merely altar boys from Jeho-vah. While the targets of some "revolutionaries" are laundramats and candy stores, Neo-HooDoo targets are TV the museums the symphony halls and churches art music and literature departments in Christianizing (education I think they call it!) universities which propogate the Art of Jeho-vah—much Byzantine Middle Ages Renaissance painting of Jeho-vah's "500 years of civilization" as Nixon put it are Jeho-vah propaganda. Many White revolutionaries can only get together with 3rd world people on the most mundane 'political' level because they are of Jeho-vah's party and don't know it. How much Black music do so called revolutionary underground radio stations play. On the other hand how much Bach?

Neo-HooDoos are Black Red (Black Hawk an American Indian was an early philosopher of the HooDoo Church) and occasionally White (Madamemoiselle Charlotte is a Haitian Loa [Spirit]).

Neo-HooDoo is a litany seeking its text
Neo-HooDoo is a Dance and Music closing in on its words
Neo-HooDoo is a Church finding its lyrics
Cecil Brown Al Young Calvin Hernton
David Henderson Steve Cannon Quincy Troupe
Ted Joans Victor Cruz N.H. Pritchard Ishmael Reed
Lennox Raphael Sarah Fabio Ron Welburn are Neo-HooDoo's "Manhattan Project" of writing . . .

A Neo-HooDoo celebration will involve the dance music and poetry of Neo-HooDoo and whatever ideas the participating artists might add. A Neo-HooDoo seal is the Face of an Old American Train.
Neo-HooDoo signs are everywhere!
Neo-HooDoo is the Now Locomotive swinging up the Tracks of the American Soul.

Almost 100 years ago HooDoo was forced to say Goodbye to America. Now HooDoo is back as Neo-HooDoo
You can't keep a good church down!

The Neo-HooDoo Aesthetic

Gombo Févi

A whole chicken—if chicken cannot be
had, veal will serve instead; a little ham;
crabs, or shrimps, or both, according to the
taste of the consumer; okra according to the
quantity of soup needed; onions, garlic, parsley
red pepper, etc. Thicken with plenty of rice.
(Don't forget to cut up the gombo or okra.)

Gombo Filé

Same as above except the okra is pul-
verised and oysters are used

Why do I call it "The Neo-HooDoo Aesthetic"?

*The proportions of ingredients used depend
upon the cook!*

Sermonette

a poet was busted by a topless judge
his friends went to morristwn nj & put
black powder on his honah's doorstep
black powder into his honah's car
black powder on his honah's briefs
tiny dolls into his honah's mind

by nightfall his honah could a go go no mo
his dog went crazy & ran into a crocodile
his widow fell from a wall &
hanged herself
his daughter was run over by a black man
cming home for the wakes the two boys
skidded into mourning
all the next of kin's teeth fell out

gimmie dat ol time
                    religion
it's good enough
        for me!

Mojo Queen of the Feathery Plumes

Why do you want me to slap you
before I make love to you, then
wonder why I do you like I do?

Dark Lady at Koptos, strange lady
at Koptos, Mojo Queen of the
Feathery Plumes.

Crawling, pleading and being
kittenish are no habits of the
world's rare cat; shut up in
the mind's dark cage; prowling
in a garden of persimmon, mangoes
and the long black python

Dark Lady at Koptos, strange lady
at Koptos, Mojo Queen of the
Feathery Plumes

When the hunter comes his gleaming
blue coat will galvanize him; his
pearls of sabre teeth will electrify
him; his avocado-green claws will
expose his guts

Dark Lady at Koptos, strange lady
at Koptos, Mojo Queen of the
Feathery Plumes.

The scout will run back thru
the forest; 4 Thieves Vinegar
on his tail; the whole safari
not far behind his trail; the dolls
left behind will bare your face;
and the cloth on the bush will be
your lace; you are the jeweler's Ruby
that has fled its case

Dark Lady at Koptos, strange lady
at Koptos, Mojo Queen of the Feathery
Plumes

The cat was dying to meet you
in the flesh but you never came
he wanted you wild but you wanted
him tame, why is your highness afraid
of the night?

Dark Lady at Koptos, strange lady at Koptos
Mojo Queen of the Feathery Plumes

The Black Cock

for Jim Hendrix, HooDoo from his natural born

He frightens all the witches and the dragons in their lair
He cues the clear blue daylight and He gives the night its dare
He flaps His wings for warning and He struts atop a mare
for when He crows they quiver and when He comes they flee

In His coal black plummage and His bright red crown
and His golden beaked fury and His calculated frown
in His webbed footed glory He sends Jehovah down
for when He crows they quiver and when He comes they flee

O they dance around the fire and they boil the gall of wolves
and they sing their strange crude melodies and play their
weirder tunes and the villagers close their windows and the
     grave-
yard starts to heave and the cross wont help their victims and
the screaming fills the night and the young girls die with
open eyes and the skies are lavender light
but when He crows they quiver and when He comes they flee

Well the sheriff is getting desperate as they go their nature's
     way
killing cattle smothering infants slaughtering those who block
     their way
and the countryside swarms with numbness as their magic
     circle grows
but when He crows they tremble and when He comes they flee

Posting hex-signs on their wagons simple worried farmers
     pray
passing laws and faking justice only feed the witches brew
violet stones are rendered helpless drunken priests are
     helpless too
but when He crows they quiver and when He comes they flee

We have seen them in their ritual we have catalogued their
     crimes
we are weary of their torture but we cannot bring them down

their ancient hoodoo enemy who does the work, the trick,
strikes peril in their dead fiend's hearts and pecks their flesh
   to quick
love Him feed Him He will never let you down
for when He crows they quiver and when He comes they frown

Betty's Ball Blues

Betty took the ring
from her fabled Jellyroll
Betty took the ring
from her fabled Jellyroll
She gave it all to Dupree
and eased it on his soul

She climbed his ancient redwood
and sang out from his peak
She climbed his ancient redwood
and sang out from his peak
She thrilled his natural forest
and made his demon creep

She shook the constellations
and dazzled them cross his eyes
She shook the constellations
and dazzled them cross his eyes
She showered his head with quasars
and made his Taurus cry

China China China
Come blow my China horn
China China China
Come blow my China horn
Telegraph my indigo skyship
and make its voyage long

Betty touched his organ
made his cathedral rock
Betty touched his organ
made his cathedral rock
His worshippers moaned
and shouted, His
stained glass windows cracked

One night she dressed
in scarlet and threw
her man a Ball
One night she dressed
in scarlet and threw
her man a Ball
The Butlers came as
zombies, the
guests walked thru
the walls

Dupree he shot the
jeweler, She had him
under a spell,
Dupree he shot the
jeweler, She had him
under a spell

The calmest man in
Sing-Sing is happy
in his cell

The Wardrobe Master of Paradise

He pins the hems of Angels and
He dresses them to kill
He has no time for fashion
No money's in His till
You wont see Him in Paris
or in a New York store
*He's the wardrobe master
of Paradise; He keeps right
on His toes*

He works from ancient patterns
He doesn't mind they bore
His models have no measurements
His buyers never roar
He never cares to gossip
He works right on the floor
*He's the wardrobe master
of Paradise; He keeps right
on His toes*

The evil cities burn to
a crisp, from where His
clients go; their eyes
are blood red carnage, their
purpose never fluffed,
His customers total seven
they have no time to pose
*He's the wardrobe master
of Paradise; He keeps right
on His toes*

He does not sweat the phony
trends, or fashions dumb
decree; His style is always
chic and in, He never takes
a fee
In Vogue or Glamour or Harper's
Bazaar; He's never written up

He's the wardrobe master
of Paradise; He keeps right
on His toes

The ups and downs of Commerce
His shop will not effect;
the whims of a fickle market
the trifles of jet-sets
The society editor would
rather die than ask Him for
a tip; He sews uninterrupted
He isn't one for quips
His light burns in the pit-black night
I've never seen Him doze
He's the wardrobe master
of Paradise; He keeps right
on His toes

catechism of d neoamerican hoodoo church

a little red wagon for d black bureaucrat
who in d winter of 1967 when i refused to
deform d works of ellison & wright—his betters—
to accommodate a viewpoint this clerk thot irresistible,
did not hire me for d teaching job
which he invitd me to take
in d first place.

this is for u insect w/ no antennae, goofy
papers piling on yr desk—for u & others. where
do u fugitives frm d file cabinet of death get
off in yr attempt to control d artist?
keep yr programming to those computers u love so
much, for he who meddles w/ nigro-mancers
courts his demise!

i

our pens are free
do not move by decree. accept no memos
frm jackbootd demogs who wd exile our minds.
dare tell d artist his role. issue demands on
cultural revolution. 2 words frm china where an
ol woman sends bold painters to pick grasshoppers
at 3 in d a.m. w/ no tea, no cigarettes & no
beer. cause ol women like landscapes or portraits
of their husbands face. done 50 yrs ago. standing
on a hill. a god, a majesty, d first chairman.
o, we who hv no dreams permit us to say yr name
all day. we are junk beneath yr feet,
mosquito noises to yr ears, we crawl on our
bellies & roll over 3 times for u. u are
definitely sho nuff d i my man.

ii

is this how artists shd greet u?
isnt yr apartment by d river enough? d
trees in d park? palisades by moonlight is
choice i hear. arent u satisfid? do u
want to be a minister of culture? (minister, a
jive title frm a dead church!) dressd in a
business suit w/ medals on yr chest? hving
painters fetch yr short, writers doing yr taxes,
musicians entertaining yr mistresses, sculptors
polishing yr silverware. do u desire 4 names
instead of 2?

iii

        i do not write solictd
    manuscripts—oswald spengler said
    to joseph goebbels when askd to make a
    lie taste like sweet milk.

because they wrote d way they saw it, said
their prayers wrong, forgot to put on their number in d
a.m., got tore dwn in d streets & cut d fool:
men changd their names to islam & hung up d phone on them.
meatheaded philosophers left rank tongues of ugly mouth on
their tables. only new/ark kept us warm that summer. but
now they will pick up d tab. those dear dead beats who put
our souls to d wall. tried us in absentia before
some grand karate who hd no style. plumes on garveys hat
he was.

iv

word of my mysteries is getting around, do not cm
said d dean / invite cancelld to speak in our chapel
at delaware state. we hv checkd yr background. u make
d crucifixes melt. d governor cant replace them.
stop   stop   outlandish customer.

v

i am becoming spooky & afar you all. i
stir in my humfo, taking notes. a black cat
superstars on my shoulder. a johnny root dwells
in my purse. on d one wall: bobs picture
of marie laveaus tomb in st louis #2. it is
all washd out w/x...s, & dead flowers &
fuck wallace signs. on d other wall:
d pastd scarab on grandpops chest, he was
a nigro-mancer frm chattanooga. so i got it
honest. i floor them w/ my gris gris. what
more do i want ask d flatfoots who patrol d beat
of my time. d whole pie? o no u small fry
spirits. d chefs hat, d kitchen, d right
to help make a menu that will end 2 thousand yrs
of bad news.

vi

muhammed? a rewrite man for d wrong daily
news. messenger for cons of d pharaohs court.
perry mason to moses d murderer & thief. pr man
for d prophets of SET. as for poets? chapt
26 my friends — check it out. it is all there in
icewater clear.

ghandi? middleclass lawyer stuck on himself.
freed d brahmins so they cd sip tea & hate cows.
lenins pants didnt fit too good,
people couldnt smoke in front of him, on d
train to petrograd he gv them passes to go
to d head.

d new houngans are to d left of buck rogers,
ok buck up w/yr hands. where did u stash
our galaxies?

vii

bulletin

        to d one who put our
art on a line. now odd shapes will nibble u.
its our turn to put u thru changes. to drop
dour walter winchells on u like, i predict
that tomorrow yr hands will be stiff. to d
one who gaggd a poet. hants will eat yr
cornflakes. golfballs will swell in yr jaws at noon.
horrid masks will gape thru yr window at dusk. it will
be an all day spectacular. look out now,
it is already beginning. to d one who strongarmd
a painter. hear d noise climbing yr steps? u will
be its horse. how does that grab u? how come u
pull d sheets over yr head? & last & least o cactus
for brains. u muggd a playwright, berkeley cal.
spring 68. We hv yr photos. lots of them. what
was that u just spat/up
a lizard or a spider?

viii

spelling out my business i hv gone
indoors. raking d coals over my liver,
listening to my stories w/ yng widow
brown, talking up a trash in bars (if
i feel up to it). doing all those things put down
in that odor of hog doodoo printd as
a poem in black fire. i caught d whiff of yr
stink thou sow w/ mud for thots. d next
round is on me. black halloween on d rocks.
straight no chaser.

down d hatch d spooks will fly / some
will thrive & some will die / by these
rattles in our hands / mighty spirits
will shake d land.

so excuse me while i do d sooner toomer.
jean that is. im gone schooner to a meta
physical country. behind d eyes. im gone be.
a rootarmd ravenheaded longbeard im gone be.
a zigaboo jazzer teaching mountain
lions of passion how to truck.

ix

goodhomefolks gave me ishmael. how
did they know he was d 'afflictd one'?
carrying a gag in his breast pocket. giving
d scene a scent of snowd under w/ bedevilment.
i am d mad mad scientist in love w/ d dark.
d villagers dont understand me. here they come
with their torches. there goes a rock
thru d window. i hv time for a few more hobbies:
making d cab drivers dream of wotan
cutting out pictures of paper murderers

like d ol woman w/ d yng face
or is it d yng woman w/ d ol face?
take yr pick. put it to my chest.
watch it bend. its all a big punchline
i share w/ u. to keep u in stitches.
& ull be so wise when their showstopper
comes:
     this is how yr ears shd feel
     this is what u shd eat
     this is who u shd sleep w/
     this is how u shd talk
     this is how u shd write
     this is how u shd paint
     these dances are d best
     these films are d best
     this is how u shd groom yrself
     these are d new gods we made for u
u are a bucket of feces before them.
we know what is best for u. bend down
& kiss some wood.
make love to leather. if u
dont u will be offd

x

& d cannd laughter will fade &
d dirty chickens will fly his coop
for he was just a geek u see.
o houngans of america — post this on yr
temples.

DO YR ART D WAY U WANT
ANYWAY U WANT
ANY WANGOL U WANT
ITS UP TO U/ WHAT WILL WORK
FOR U.

41

so sez d neoarmerican hoodoo
church of free spirits who
need no
monarch
no gunghoguru
no busybody ray frm d heddahopper planet
of wide black hats & stickpins. he was
just a 666* frm a late late show &
only d clucks threw pennies

* false prophet of the apocalypse

why i often allude to osiris

ikhnaton looked like
prophet jones , who brick
by brick broke up a
french chateau & set it
down in detroit . he was
'elongated' like prophet
jones & had a hairdresser's
taste .
ikhnaton moved cities for
his mother-in-law &
each finger of his hands
bore rings .

ikhnaton brought re
ligious fascism to egypt .

where once man animals
plants & stars freely
roamed thru each other's
rooms , ikhnaton came up
with the door .

(a lot of people in new york
   go for him—museum curators
   politicians & tragic mulattoes)

i'll take osiris any
time .
prefiguring JB he
funky chickened into
ethiopia & everybody had
a good time . osiris in
vented the popcorn , the
slow drag & the lindy hop .

he'd rather dance than rule .

my thing abt cats

in berkeley whenever
black cats saw dancer &
me they crossed over to
the other side . alan &
carol's cat jumped over
my feet . someone else's
cat pressed it's paw against
my leg . in seattle it's
green eyes all the way .
"they cry all the time when
ever you go out, but when
you return they stop ," dancer
said of the 3 cats in the back
yard on st mark's place . there
is a woman downstairs who makes
their sounds when she feeds them .
we don't get along .

man or butterfly

it is like lao tse's dream , my
strange affair with cities .
sometimes i can't tell whether
i am a writer writing abt cities
or a city with cities writing
abt me .
a city in peril . everything that
makes me tick is on the bum . all
of my goods and services are wearing
down . nothing resides in me anymore .
i am becoming a ghost town with not
even an occasional riot to perk me
up

                they are setting up a
                commission to find out what
                is wrong with me . i
                am the lead off witness

hoodoo poem in transient

Ince a year marie laveau
    rises frm her workshop
    in st louis #2 , boards
    a bus & rides dwn to
    the lake . she threw
    parties there 100 years
    ago .
    some
    lake

Monsters From
The Ozarks

The Gollygog
The Bingbuffer
The Moogie
The Fillyloo
The Behemoth
The Snawfus
The Gowrow
The Spiro
The Agnew

beware: do not read this poem

tonite , *thriller* was
abt an ol woman , so vain she
surrounded her self w/
    many mirrors

it got so bad that finally she
locked herself indoors & her
whole life became the
    mirrors

one day the villagers broke
into her house , but she was too
swift for them . she disappeared
    into a mirror
each tenant who bought the house
after that , lost a loved one to
    the ol woman in the mirror :
    first a little girl
    then a young woman
    then the young woman/s husband

the hunger of this poem is legendary
it has taken in many victims
back off from this poem
it has drawn in yr feet
back off from this poem
it has drawn in yr legs
back off from this poem
it is a greedy mirror
you are into this poem . from
    the waist down
nobody can hear you can they ?
this poem has had you up to here
    belch
this poem aint got no manners
you cant call out frm this poem
relax now & go w/ this poem
move & roll on to this poem

do not resist this poem
this poem has yr eyes
this poem has his head
this poem has his arms
this poem has his fingers
this poem has his fingertips

this poem is the reader & the
reader this poem

statistic : the us bureau of missing persons reports
that in 1968 over 100,000 people disappeared
leaving no solid clues
nor trace   only
a space   in the lives of their friends

Dualism

in ralph ellison's invisible man

i am outside of
history. i wish
i had some peanuts, it
looks hungry there in
its cage

i am inside of
history. its
hungrier than i
thot

Guilty, the New York Philharmonic
Signs Up a Whale

Today the New York
Philharmonic signed up
a whale.
Ortiz Walton is black
& better than Casals.
Well Ortiz, I guess you'll
have to swim the Atlantic

if my enemy is a clown,
a natural born clown

i tore down my thoughts
roped in my nightmares
remembered a thousand curses
made blasphemous vows to demons
choked on the blood of hosts
        ate my hat
threw fits in the street
got up bitchy each day
told off the mailman
lost many friends
left parties in a huff
dry fucked a dozen juke boxes
made anarchist speeches in brad
the falcon's 55 (but was never
thrown out)
drank 10 martinis a minute
until 1 day the book was finished

my unspeakable terror between the
covers, on you i said to the
enemies of the souls

well lorca, pushkin i tried
but in this place they assasinate
you with pussy or pats on
the back. lemon chiffon between
the cheeks or 2 weeks on a mile
long beach.

i have been the only negro
on the plane 10 times this year
and its only the 2nd month

i am removing my blindfold and
leaving the dock. the judge
giggles constantly and the prosecutor
invited me to dinner

no forwarding address please

i called it pin the tail on the devil
they called it avant garde
they just can't be serious
these big turkeys

the piping down of god

god is above grammar
a monk once said . i
want to sit on the window
god told the ticket clerk . you
mean next to the window the
clerk corrected . no , on
the window god insisted . the
clouds have a right to
cheer their boss .

the clerk apologized
& god piped down .

Anon. Poster:

poor sam presents at

ESTHER'S ORBIT ROOM

1753–7th Street Oakland California
Reunion of Soul
with the Sensational Team of
Vernon & Jewel
(back together again)
music by
the Young Lyons

american airlines sutra

put yr cup on my tray
the stewardess said 40,000
feet up . (well i've
never done it that way . what
have i got to lose .)

i climb into a cab & the
woman driver is singing
along with Frank Sinatra
" how was your flight coming in ? "

(another one . these americans ,
only one thing on their
minds) .

the inside track

a longshot if he cracks up in
doors, but 2 to 1 he
flips out on tv. every
time nixon goes before the
cameras, 80,000 bookies
hold their breaths

who hated voo doo

for cardinal spellman

sick
black grass will
grow on his plot and
the goats will eat
and choke on it

and the keeper of the children's
cries
will terrify his neighbors
& gravediggers
will ask for two weeks
off

when will the next one's
brain explode
or turn from meat to
rock

tomorrow
a week
a month from someday
or the next three turns
of the
moon

dragon's blood

just because you
cant see d stones dont
mean im not building .
you aint no mason . how
d fuck would you know .

columbia

a dumb
figure
skater per
forming to
strauss'
*also spake
zarathustra* .

she stumbled
during the spin .

i saw this today
on wide wide
world of
sports .

no lie .

treatment for dance w/ trick ending

one cop enters a store
a 2nd cop pulls a cat frm a tree
a 3rd cop helps an ol woman across
    the street
a 4th cop slaps a prisoner

the cop who pulled the cat frm the
tree leaves the store with a package
& whistling walks dwn the street
the prisoner is put into a box away frm
his fellows
the ol woman files a complaint

one nite in 1965 at 3 in the AM i
stumble down second ave.
8 cadillacs pull up in front
of ratner's . it is a shift of
the 9th precinct . coming on duty
the next morning the cobbler
awakes to find his shoes ruined

Back to Back : 3rd Eye

for D.H.

Who are you ? Napoleon or something ? Fresh from Elba ,
liberating the countryside ? You wonder why cheering throngs
don't turn out to greet you , in Oakland , in Richmond , in El
Cerrito , behind the county courthouse on the telephone
book . New York will follow you like a Westside meatpacking
house that barters your heart for free ice . They keep to themselves out here .

        Marlon Brando's silver hair sells
        Up-America cakes on the weekends .

    STOP !

Western Union for Zora Neale Hurston :
*Moscow has fallen ! Please wire Erzulie for triumphant
march into the art!*

off d pig

for f duvalier who maintained
d trust

background:
    a reckoning has left
some minds hard hit . they blow ,
crying for help , out to sea like
dead trees & receding housetops . i
can sympathize . i mean , all of us
have had our dreams broken over some
body's head . those scratched phono
graph records of d soul .
we
      all have been zombed along
d way of a thousand eyes glowing at midnite .
      our pupils have been vacant
      our hands have been icey &
      we have walked with d tell tale
      lurch
all of us have had this crisis of consciousness
which didnt do nobody no good
or a search for identity
which didnt make no never mind neither

at those times we got down on our knees & call
ed up the last resort . seldom do we bother him
for he is doing heavy duty for d universe . only
once has he been disturbed & this was to
    put some color into a woman's blues
he came like a black fire engine spun & sped
by khepera
he is very pressed for time &
do nots play

he apologises for being late
he rolls up his sleeves & rests his bird
he starts to say a few words to d crowd .
he sees d priests are out to lunch so he
just goes on head with what he got to do

63

out of d night blazing from ceciltaylorpianos
   Thoth sets down his fine black self
d first black scribe
d one who fixes up their art
d one who draws d circle with his pen
d man who beats around d bush
d smeller outer of d fiend

        jehovah-apep jumps up bad on d set
        but squeals as spears bring him down

a curfew is lifted on soul
friendly crowds greet one another in d streets
Osiris struts his stuff & dos d thang to words
    hidden beneath d desert

chorus—just like a legendary train that
       one has heard of but never seen
       broke all records in its prime
       takes you where you want to go right fast

       i hears you woo woo o neo american hoo doo church
       i hears you woo woo o neo american hoo doo church
       i hears you woo woo o neo american hoo doo church
       i hears you woo woo o neo american hoo doo church
       amen-ra   a-men ra   a- man ra

General Science

things in motion
hv a tendency to
stay in motion . the
most intelligent
ghost are those
who do not know
they are dead:

something just
crossed my
hands

Report of the
Reed Commission

i conclude that for
the first time in
history the practical
man is the loon and the
loon the practical man

a man on the radio just
said that air pollution
is caused by jelly fish .

what you mean
i cant irony ?

A high-yellow lawyer woman
told me i ought to go to
Europe to " broaden your per
spective ." This happened at
a black black cocktail party
an oil portrait , Andrew Carnegie ,
smiling down

white hope

for shane stevens

jack johnson licked
one pug so , d man
retired to a farm .
never again opened
his mouth save to
talk abt peachtrees
sow & last year's
almanac ;

and whenever somebody
say jack johnson ,

he'd get that far away
look .

Untitled I

friday in berkeley . the crippled
ship has just returned frm
behind the moon . fools wave
flags on destroyers in the pacific
i am worried abt this dog
lying in the street . he wants
to get some sun . the old man
across the street trims his
rosebush while just 4 blocks
away there is a war . people
are being arraigned
fingerprinted
hauled away to st rita
made to lie on the floor
the newspapers will lie
abt all this . abt these
12 year olds throwing
stones at the cops . they
wanted to get at some sun
no matter what heavy
traffic was coming down
on them

Untitled II

that house has
a pall of bad
luck hovering over
head
i told you
not to go there
anymore . see
what you get ?

Untitled III

everybody in columbia
heights speaks french
ever go to a party there ?
bore you to tears .

Untitled IV

the difference between
my heart & your
intellect , my un
disciplined way of
doing
things (i failed
the written driver's
test for example)
& your science , is
the difference between
the earth &
the snow .

the earth wears its
colors well . builds them
loves them & sticks with
them

the snow needs no one .
it lies there all cold
like . it greases behind
wolftracks & wingless
dead birds .
it is a hardship on the poor

thinking is its downfall

Gangster Goes Legit

One day he became six eyes.
The tommy gun on the desk,
as many.
he went into the tommy gun
business

this poetry anthology
i'm reading

this poetry anthology
i'm reading reminds me
of washington d.c.
every page some marbled
trash . old adjectives stand
next to flagcovered coffins .
murderers mumbling in
their sleep .

in the rose garden the
madman strolls alone . the
grin on his face just
won't quit

dress rehearsal paranoia #2

in san francisco they are
taking up a collection . if
the earthquake won't come
they'll send for it .

Paul Lawrence Dunbar
in The Tenderloin

Even at 26 , the hush when
you unexpectedly walked
into a theatre . One year
after *The History of Cakewalk* .

Desiring not to cause
a fuss , you sit alone
in the rear , watching a re
hearsal .
The actors are impressed . Wel
don Johnson , so super at des
cription , jots it all down .

I dont blame you for
disliking Whitman , Paul .
He lacked your style , like
your highcollared mandalaed
portrait in hayden's
Kaleidoscope ; unobserved ,
Death , the uncouth critic
does a first draft on your
     breath .

Badman of the guest professor

for joe overstreet, david henderson, albert ayler
& d mysterious 'H' who cut up d rembrandts

i

u worry me whoever u are
i know u didnt want me to
come here but here i am just
d same; hi-jacking yr stagecoach,
hauling in yr pocket watches & mak
ing u hoof it all d way to
town. black bard, a robber w/ an
art: i left some curses in d cash
box so ull know its me

listen man, i cant help it if
yr thing is over, kaput,
    finis
no matter how u slice it dick
u are done. a dead duck all out
of quacks. d nagging hiccup dat
goes on & on w/out a simple glass
    of water for relief

ii

uve been teaching shakespeare for
20 years only to find d joke
        on u
d eavesdropping rascal who got it
in d shins because he didnt know
enough to keep his feet behind d cur
tains: a sad-sacked head served on a
platter in titus andronicus or falstaff
        too fat to make a go of it
        anymore

77

iii

its not my fault dat yr tradition
was knocked off wop style & left in
d alley w/ pricks in its mouth. i
read abt it in d papers but it was no
        skin off my nose
wasnt me who opened d gates & allowed
d rustlers to slip thru unnoticed. u
ought to do something abt yr security or
        mend yr fences partner
dont look at me if all dese niggers
are ripping it up like deadwood dick;
doing art d way its never been done. mak
ing wurlitzer sorry he made d piano dat
will drive mozart to d tennis
        courts
making smith-corona feel like d red
faced university dat has just delivered china
        some 50 e-leben h bomb experts

i didnt deliver d blow dat drove d
abstract expressionists to my ladies
linoleum where dey sleep beneath tons of
wax & dogshit & d muddy feet of children or
because some badassed blackpainter done sent
french impressionism to d walls of highrise
        lobbies where dey belong is not my fault
martha graham will never do d jerk
shes a sweet ol soul but her hips
cant roll; as stiff as d greek
statues she loves so much

iv

dese are d reasons u did me nasty
j alfred prufrock, d trick u pull
d in d bookstore today; stand in d
corner no peaches for a week, u lemon

u must blame me because yr wife is
ugly. 86-d by a thousand discriminating
saunas. dats why u did dat sneaky thing
i wont tell d townsfolk because u hv
to live here and im just passing thru

v

u got one thing right tho. i did say
dat everytime i read william faulkner i
go to sleep.

fitzgerald wdnt hv known a gangster if one
had snatchd zelda & made her a moll tho
        she wd hv been grateful i bet

bonnie of clyde wrote d saga of suicide
sal just as d feds were closing in. it is
worth more than d collected works of ts
eliot a trembling anglican whose address
is now d hell dat thrilld him so
last word from down there he was open
ing a publishing co dat will bore d
devil back to paradise

vi

& by d way did u hear abt grammar?
cut to ribbons in a photo finish by
stevie wonder, a blindboy who dances
on a heel. he just came out of d slang
& broke it down before millions.
      it was bloody murder

vii

to make a long poem shorter – 3 things
      moleheaded lame w/4 or 5 eyes

1) yr world is riding off into d sunset
2) d chips are down & nobody will chance yr i.o.u.s
3) d last wish was a fluke so now u hv to re
turn to being a fish
p.s. d enchantment has worn off

dats why u didnt like my reading list – right?
it didnt include anyone on it dat u cd in
vite to a cocktail party & shoot a lot of
      bull – right?
so u want to take it out on my hide – right?
well i got news for u professor nothing – i
am my own brand while u must be d fantasy of
      a japanese cartoonist

a strangekind of dinosaurmouse
i can see it all now. d leaves
are running low. its d eve of
extinction & dere are no holes to
accept yr behind. u wander abt yr
long.neck probing a tree. u think
its a tree but its really a trap. a
cry of victory goes up in d kitchen of

d world. a pest is dead. a prehis
toric pest at dat. a really funnytime
prehistoric pest whom we will lug into
a museum to show everyone how really funny
u are
         yr fate wd make a good
scenario but d plot is between u &
charles darwin. u know, whitefolkese
         business

as i said, im passing thru, just sing
ing my song. get along little doggie &
jazz like dat. word has it dat a big gold
shipment is coming to californy. i hv to
ride all night if im to meet my pardners
dey want me to help score d ambush

from the files of
agent 22

a black banana
can make you high
bad apples can get
you wasted
the wrong kind of
grapes tore up
for days
and a rancid orange
plastered

know your spirits
before entering
strange orchards

introducing a new loa

as i conclude this Work , a great hydrogen cloud , twenty seven million miles long leisurely passes thru this solar system at 40,000 miles per hr . '' The biggest thing yet seen in space . '' No one knows where it came from . Another galaxy ? This solar system ?

it took the small halo of another planet, out to make a rep for itself , to squeal on it . I claim it as my floating orphan . When i walked past the FM antenna just now , it called out my name . I respond to it . I call it the invisible train for which this Work has been but a modest schedule . A time-table subject to change . Greetings from the swinging HooDoo cloud ; way up there , the softest touch in Everything ; doing a dance they call
"The Our Turn"